Our Journey Into Eternity

Dr. Telford Barrett

Xulon
PRESS

Our Journey Into Eternity
by Dr. Telford Barrett

Printed in the United States of America

ISBN 978-1-60791-188-3

www.xulonpress.com

BOOK ONE

THE CHRISTIAN'S JOURNEY INTO ETERNITY

BOOK TWO

THE LOST PERSONS JOURNEY INTO ETERNITY

PREFACE

When a Christian dies they are guided by the angels to Heaven where God dwells. The Lord Jesus is there to receive His bride who will forever enjoy His love and care for them. All New Testament believers will never be separated from Jesus who will continually reveal His love to His bride forever.

Jesus will bring His Church back to this earth, after the tribulation period, and set up one thousand years of rule and reign over the earth with believers ruling and reigning with him. At the end of the millennium Jesus will create a new Heaven and a new earth where we will dwell for all eternity.

Many believe a person qualifies to go to heaven by being good. There are many who also believe you go to hell if you commit enough sins to out weigh the good works you have done. There is only one sin that condemns a soul to the lake of fire and that is by refusing to receive Jesus as their lord and Saviour. God has always required a proper atonement for the forgiveness of sins. Jesus made the final atonement in which God the Father was completely satisfied. God forgives all sins. We who by faith must accept the atonement Jesus made to be received into Heaven when we die. There is a separation of the saved from the lost people when they die. The saved are taken to Heaven and the lost go down into Hades.

BOOK ONE

THE CHRISTIAN'S JOURNEY
INTO ETERNITY

CHAPTER ONE

THE BELIEVERS VICTORY OVER DEATH:

When a person receives Christ as their Lord and Savior, their soul is saved by the atonement made by Jesus when He died on the cross. The human body with the Adamic sinful nature, we inherited from Adam, cannot enter into Heaven with that body. It is necessary for every Christian to lay aside this sinful flesh and have a form appropriate to stand in the presence of a Holy God. I Cor.15:50.

When a Christian dies their soul, or heart, goes immediately into Heaven and then into the presence of the Lord Jesus who saved them

2Co 5:8 We are confident, *I say*, and willing rather to be absent from the body, and to be present with the Lord.

When Jesus was using the illustration of Lazarus and the rich man He informed those around Him that an Angel took the soul of Lazarus and carried it into the third Heaven where God dwells. It is a tremendous comfort to learn from this scripture that Believers will not have to find their way into Heaven alone. Luke 16:22. The new form that is given to believers is that of a Spirit much like that of Angels. The form angels have is far superior to that of a human body. Christians who have a resurrected body will have authority over angels and above them by being a Christian who will be the Bride of Christ when we get to Heaven.

1Co 6:3 Know ye not that we shall judge angels? how much more things that pertain to this life? 1Co 15:50 Now this I say, brethren, that flesh and blood cannot inherit the kingdom of God; neither doth corruption inherit incorruption.

Angels have great power, able to do any thing God requests of them, and also to comfort and guard believers while they live on earth.

It is quite obvious that believers who are in their spirit form will have a superior intellect more than we now have on earth.

There will be Christians alive when Jesus comes near to the earth to gather His bride to take them to Heaven. Those alive at His coming will not experience a natural death like those who died before this time; they will exchange this natural flesh and put on a glorious body like that of those who are resurrected from the grave. The next move for this body is for the Lord to take us to the third Heaven where God dwells. The action of this transformation will take place in a fraction of a second and those who have been changed, with a new heavenly body, will then join other believers and meet the Lord Jesus in the air. The next move for this body is for the Lord to take us to the third Heaven where God dwells.

1Co 15:51 Behold, I shew you a mystery; We shall not all sleep, but we shall all be changed,

1Co 15:52 In a moment, in the twinkling of an eye, at the last trump: for the trumpet shall sound, and the dead shall be raised incorruptible, and we shall be changed.

1Co 15:53 For this corruptible must put on incorruption, and this mortal *must* put on immortality.

KNOWLEDGE ABOUT THINGS ON EARTH:

There is not any information in the Bible that would indicate Christians, who are in Heaven, are able to communicate with people still alive on earth. Some individuals have claimed to communicate with the dead but no proof has ever been found to verify this to be true. In Luke 16:19-31 some information is given about the rich man in Hades who had an understanding about the place of suffering he was experiencing. Also, the rich man recognized others who were there and about his brothers who were still alive. The rich man in Hades asked Abraham to send some one back to the earth to warn his brothers not to come to this place of suffering. Abraham informed the rich man that no one could leave that place and warn others about Hades.

SAINTS IN HEAVEN KNOW WHEN OTHERS ARE SAVED:

We would love to think that our departed loved ones who are now in Heaven know what is happening to us back on earth. The Bible does not reveal how much the Saints in Heaven know about things on earth. The only information recorded in the Bible about those in Heaven knowing about what is happening on earth is found in Luke 15:10. Scripture gives us clear information that departed Saints will forever be in the presence of Angels. Those who are in the presence of angels would have to be those who are Christians in Heaven and have learned about those who are dear to them still on earth and have trusted Jesus to save them. The Joy experienced by the Heavenly Saints is the result of learning about their loved ones on earth who have trusted Jesus to save them. Luke 15:10 also teaches us that those in Heaven have emotions of joy as a result of the good news they have learned from Angels.

Luk 15:10 Likewise, I say unto you, there is joy in the presence of the angels of God over one sinner that repenteth.

13

It may be possible for those in Heaven to know much about what is happening to people back on earth, but Scripture does not give further information about that.

THE DWELLING PLACE FOR CHRISTIANS IN HEAVEN:

The comforting words of Jesus was a blessing for all Christians when He told His disciples he was going away to Heaven and prepare for us a mansion. The splendor and beauty of this dwelling place that the Lord is building for us is beyond human description.

The location of our Heavenly home, at this time, is in the third Heaven where God the Father, the Son, and Holy Spirit now dwell.

Joh 14:1 Let not your heart be troubled: ye believe in God, believe also in me.

Joh 14:2 In my Father's house are many mansions: if *it were* not *so*, I would have told you. I go to prepare a place for you.

Joh 14:3 And if I go and prepare a place for you, I will come again, and receive you unto myself; that where I am, *there* ye may be also.

The following verse is a blessing to all Christians who think about Heaven and our Heavenly Home.

1Co 2:9 But as it is written, Eye hath not seen, nor ear heard, neither have entered into the heart of man, the things which God hath prepared for them that love him.

ALL CHRISTIANS ARE TAKEN TO HEAVEN:

The disciples asked Jesus to tell them when He will return to the earth and take the elect to Heaven. Jesus instructed the disciples saying to be careful about following false teachers who will set dates about the time for the coming of Jesus to take His Church to Heaven.

> Mat 24:3 And as he sat upon the mount of Olives, the disciples came unto him privately, saying, Tell us, when shall these things be? and what *shall be* the sign of thy coming, and of the end of the world?

> Mat 24:4 And Jesus answered and said unto them, Take heed that no man deceive you.

If Jesus had given the date for his return, many believers would not prepare for his coming until that date arrived. Jesus knew that if we did not know the time of His return, this would be an incentive for believers to be ready for Jesus to return at any time. Mat 24:44 Therefore be ye also ready: for in such an hour as ye think not the Son of man cometh.

Jesus illustrated His coming again to be like that of a thief -you do not expect. Jesus will come when most people do not expect Him.

> - Luk 12:39 And this know, that if the goodman of the house had known what hour the thief would come, he would have watched, and not have suffered his house to be broken through.

Jesus chose not to know the time of His return so He could truthfully say to His disciples that He did not know the time of His return. At this time God only knew of the time Jesus would return for His Bride.

> Mar 13:32 But of that day and *that* hour knoweth no man, no, not the angels which are in heaven, neither the Son, but the Father.

THE DAY OF OUR RESURRECTION:

Jesus will leave Heaven and bring the souls of Christians who have already died with Him. Jesus will draw near to the earth and remain in the air to receive His Bride. An Archangel will call for the bodies of Christians in the grave to arise first. The trump of God will also sound with such intensity that the atmosphere around the earth will reverberate perhaps like that of thunder.

1Th 4:16 For the Lord himself shall descend from heaven with a shout, with the voice of the archangel, and with the trump of God: and the dead in Christ shall rise first:

All the saints of God who have died during this dispensation of Grace will come forth out of the grave with a glorified body like that of Jesus when He was resurrected. Our Spirit form, which has been in Heaven since our death, will now be placed into the resurrected body.

Phi 3:21 Who shall change our vile body, that it may be fashioned like unto his glorious body, according to the working whereby he is able even to subdue all things unto himself.

Those who have died will have their atoms brought together and reconstructed into a glorified new body without the Adamic sinful nature we now possess. Since we now have a resurrected body like that of Jesus, it may not be necessary for our graves to be opened for us to leave the grave. Jesus with his glorified resurrected body entered the upper room, to meet with the disciples, without opening the door proving that any material substance does not hold Him.

Joh 20:19 Then the same day at evening, being the first *day* of the week, when the doors were shut where the disciples were assembled for fear of the Jews, came Jesus and stood in the midst, and saith unto them, Peace *be* unto you.

Believers will have a resurrected glorified body that will have the same likeness to that of the body of Jesus. No material of any type can hold the resurrected body of Christians from meeting the Lord in the air.

TOGETHER WE WILL MEET THE LORD IN THE AIR:

The next prophesy to be fulfilled will be the catching away of the New Testament Church to meet their Saviour in the air and then to be taken into Heaven.

1Th 4:14 For if we believe that Jesus died and rose again, even so them also which sleep in Jesus will God bring with him.

I Th 4:15 For this we say unto you by the word of the Lord, that we which are alive *and* remain unto the coming of the Lord shall not prevent them which are asleep.

1Th 4:16 For the Lord himself shall descend from heaven with a shout, with the voice of the archangel, and with the trump of God: and the dead in Christ shall rise first:

1Th 4:17 Then we which are alive *and* remain shall be caught up together with them in the clouds, to meet the Lord in the air: and so shall we ever be with the Lord.

1Th 4:18 Wherefore comfort one another with these words.

There is a good possibility there will be a short period of time for us to greet our loved ones for a blessed reunion. Quickly we will then be caught up into the atmosphere to meet the Lord Jesus who saved us by His grace. From this event there will never be a moment of time when we will be separated from our Saviour and our loved ones.

CHAPTER TWO

ENTERING HEAVEN WHERE GOD DWELLS:

The meeting in the air will be the beginning of our move into the third Heaven where we will be able to see God the Father on His throne. After the Bride of Christ receives a glorified body they will be able to see clearly the physical form of all spiritual bodies such as angels and God who is a Spirit. Today we have limited ability and can only see material things. In Heaven, Christians will have unlimited sight and now be able to see all things in Heaven. Believers will all gather around the Throne of God with Jesus at His right hand and worship God with an exceeding joyful praise beyond any thing we could ever Imagine. This anthem of praise will continue forever. This exaltation will never cease because our God will always be worthy of such praise.

> Rev 4:11 Thou art worthy, O Lord, to receive glory and honour and power: for thou hast created all things, and for thy pleasure they are and were created.

THE BRILLIANT LIGHTS IN HEAVEN:

When the saint of God first arrives in Heaven, they will be dazzled by the brilliant colors that will fill all of Heaven. God is light and light of its purest form will shine forth from His Holy nature. Believers in their resurrected body will now be able to see the Heavenly lights in the full spectrum of colors. We will experience light never known on this earth.

1Jo 1:5 This then is the message which we have heard of him, and declare unto you, that God is light, and in him is no darkness at all.

The new home, for the Bride of Christ, is called The Holy Jerusalem.
John in the Book of Revelation describes the light of that Heavenly Home to be the glory of God.

Rev 21:10 And he carried me away in the spirit to a great and high mountain, and shewed me that great city, the holy Jerusalem, descending out of heaven from God,

Rev 21:11 Having the glory of God: and her light was like unto a stone most precious, even like a jasper stone, clear as crystal;

John further describes the lights of heaven with their gleam of different colors of light which shine from precious jewels. The brilliance each jewel emits will excite all who sees those colors. In Heaven the source of light will now be the pure light of God's glory and the reflection of many colors will take on the illustrious colors that is beyond human description.
When a person views the Royal Jewels and Crowns of England they are awed by the brilliant colors from the jewels. It is beyond any human language to be able to describe the scene around the throne of God, with the brilliant light of God shinning upon our crowns, we will place these crowns before the throne of Jesus after they have been awarded to us at the Judgment Seat.

Rev 21:11 Having the glory of God: and her light *was* like unto a stone most precious, even like a jasper stone, clear as crystal;

Rev 4:10 The four and twenty elders fall down before him that sat on the throne, and worship him that liveth for ever and ever, and cast their crowns before the throne, saying,

Rev 4:11 Thou art worthy, O Lord, to receive glory and honour and power: for thou hast created all things, and for thy pleasure they are and were created.

BELIEVERS WILL RECOGNIZE EACH OTHER IN HEAVEN:

When we receive our glorified body it will be like the body Jesus had when he came out of the tomb on Easter Morning. The resurrected body of Jesus was able to move from this earth into Heaven because gravity had no power to hold Him. Material substance could not restrict His movements into a closed room.

Act 1:9 And when he had spoken these things, while they beheld, he was taken up; and a cloud received him out of their sight.

Act 1:10 And while they looked stedfastly toward heaven as he went up, behold, two men stood by them in white apparel;

Act 1:11 Which also said, Ye men of Galilee, why stand ye gazing up into heaven? this same Jesus, which is taken up from you into heaven, shall so come in like manner as ye have seen him go into heaven.

Joh 20:19 Then the same day at evening, being the first *day* of the week, when the doors were shut where the disciples were assembled for fear of the Jews, came Jesus and stood in the midst, and saith unto them, Peace *be* unto you.

Peter recognized Jesus after His resurrection. Jesus was preparing food for the hungry disciples who had been fishing. During the twilight, their boat was drawing near to land and at some distance the disciples recognized Jesus because He looked the same as He did before He was crucified. Those in the upper room immediately recognized Jesus as He entered the closed room.

> Joh 21:12 Jesus saith unto them, Come *and* dine. And none of the disciples durst ask him, Who art thou? knowing that it was the Lord.

> Joh 21:13 Jesus then cometh, and taketh bread, and giveth them, and fish likewise.

> Joh 21:14 This is now the third time that Jesus shewed himself to his disciples, after that he was risen from the dead.

After we are resurrected we shall be like Jesus and have the same ability and physical features that we had before our death. Jesus was about thirty three years old when He was resurrected from the tomb; If we are going to be like Jesus when He was resurrected there is a good possibility that we will also look to be about thirty three years of age. All the imperfections of our body will be removed and our features will also be that age of thirty three. Recognizing each other by features we had before death will be a tremendous blessing to know our loved ones as we knew them on earth. All infants and children who died prematurely will be resurrected and look like they would have appeared had they lived to be thirty years of age.

> Phi 3:21 Who shall change our vile body, that it may be fashioned like unto his glorious body, according to the working whereby he is able even to subdue all things unto himself.

THE JUDGMENT SEAT OF CHRIST:

The judgment of Believers will take place soon after we arrive in Heaven with our glorified body.

2Co 5:8 We are confident, *I say*, and willing rather to be absent from the body, and to be present with the Lord.

The Judgment seat does not determine if we go to Heaven or not. All of our sins were judged at Calvary and it will not ever be necessary to judge Believers again for their sins. The primary reason for this trial is to determine if we have lived a life on earth for the glory of our Lord Jesus. Paul gives a reason for living a successful Christian life which was to hear the approval of Jesus when he enters Heaven.

2Ti 4:7 I have fought a good fight, I have finished *my* course, I have kept the faith:

2Ti 4:8 Henceforth there is laid up for me a crown of righteousness, which the Lord, the righteous judge, shall give me at that day: and not to me only, but unto all them also that love his appearing.

The Judgment Seat was placed on an elevated place so the judge could see those who participated in the sports events.. The Apostle Paul used this place for an illustration where a judge would sit and determine who was the winner of their event and then they would receive as a reward, the winner's crown. Those who lost the race would not be punished; they would only loose the reward of receiving a crown.

All Believers will stand before the Lord Jesus to be judged for our works done while we lived on earth.

2Co 5:10 For we must all appear before the judgment seat of Christ; that every one may receive the things *done* in *his* body, according to that he hath done, whether *it be* good or bad.

Believers will not be judged for the talent they are given by the Lord.

Every Christian will be judged for their faithfulness in doing the ministry of service the Lord has called them to do.

1Co 3:12 Now if any man build upon this foundation gold, silver, precious stones, wood, hay, stubble;

1Co 3:13 Every man's work shall be made manifest: for the day shall declare it, because it shall be revealed by fire; and the fire shall try every man's work of what sort it is.

1Co 3:14 If any man's work abide which he hath built thereupon, he shall receive a reward.

1Co 3:15 If any man's work shall be burned, he shall suffer loss: but he himself shall be saved; yet so as by fire.

The little things we do for others to glorify the Lord Jesus will not be forgotten and will be rewarded.

Mat 10:42 And whosoever shall give to drink unto one of these little ones a cup of cold *water* only in the name of a disciple, verily I say unto you, he shall in no wise lose his reward.

REWARDS WILL BE GIVEN TO THE FAITHFUL:

The Holy Spirit moved Paul to write instructing Believers that performing their talent for the purpose of bringing glory to the Lord Jesus will be material like gold and silver which will be judged at the Judgment Seat and be rewarded accordingly.

Rom 14:10 But why dost thou judge thy brother? or why dost thou set at nought thy brother? for we shall all stand before the judgment seat of Christ.

Paul describes the reward as being a crown and added Jewels for many good works.

Christians who fail to use their talent of service for the glory of God will not receive any crowns, as a reward for selfish service in this life.

Works Believers do for the acclaim of man will be destroyed as unacceptable to Jesus; as a result there will be no crowns given to that child of God.

2Ti 4:8 Henceforth there is laid up for me a crown of righteousness, which the Lord, the righteous judge, shall give me at that day: and not to me only, but unto all them also that love his appearing.

Five crowns are recorded in Scripture that may be received:

1. Incorruptible Crown - I Cor. 9:25
2. Crown of Rejoicing – I Thess. 2:19
3. Crown of Life – James 1:12
4. Crown of Righteousness – II Tim. 4:8
5. Crown of Glory – I Peter 5:4

Every good deed performed by a Christian is the result of God's grace being worked out through all Believers. It is still true that all works of the flesh are like filthy rags in the sight of God. Any good work any one does is the result of God working through them. The only thing we can do is to be willing for the Holy Spirit to work through us to do the will of God.

After the rewards are given to Believers in Heaven, it appears that they with the twenty four Elders will place their crown before the throne located in the center of Heaven. The reason this will be done is all Christians will realize what they have been able to do was the result of what Christ has done through them. Placing the crowns with all of their Jewels reflecting the pure light of God's Glory will be a scene of beauty that will add to the glory of the One who saved us.

The rewards earned at the Judgment Seat will determine our office of rule during the thousand years of rule over this world during the millennial reign of Jesus who will rule from the Throne of David in Jerusalem. The greater the reward at the Judgment Seat will result in a greater position of ruling with Christ over the earth during the millennium. The office of rule during the millennium will be a monarchy with Jesus on the throne and all other positions of rule will be under His command.

> Rev 20:6 Blessed and holy *is* he that hath part in the first resurrection: on such the second death hath no power, but they shall be priests of God and of Christ, and shall reign with him a thousand years.

Jesus was the first to be resurrected from the dead and receive a glorified body. We have apart in that first resurrection by accepting the death, burial, and resurrection of the Lord Jesus Christ. It is important for all Believers to trust God, as long as they live, to do all of the good works Jesus has enabled us to do. 2Ti 4:6 For I am now ready to be offered, and the time of my departure is at hand.

> 2Ti 4:7 I have fought a good fight, I have finished *my* course, I have kept the faith:

Every Christian who is very faithful to perform their little talent God has given them will be rewarded an important place of rule in the Millennium. A Believer will not be rewarded for the talent he has been given; rewards are given because of their faithfulness to perform their ministry God has given them.

> Luk 19:17 And he said unto him, Well, thou good servant: because thou hast been faithful in a very little, have thou authority over ten cities.

THE MARRIAGE OF THE LAMB:

After the rewards are given to the New Testament Church, who is the Bride of Christ, will be united to Christ and become one with Him. The marriage will take place in the Father's home. A custom in Israel during the Old Testament period was for the bride to go to the home of the father of the bridegroom for the wedding. The wedding ceremony was a private event with the family present. The New Testament Believers are now in Heaven, which is the Father's House, and will be united to Christ Jesus forever as His bride. This wedding also will be attended only by the Trinity and the Angels.

> Rev 19:7 Let us be glad and rejoice, and give honour to him: for the marriage of the Lamb is come, and his wife hath made herself ready.

> Rev 19:8 And to her was granted that she should be arrayed in fine linen, clean and white: for the fine linen is the righteousness of saints.

> Rev 19:9 And he saith unto me, Write, Blessed *are* they which are called unto the marriage supper of the Lamb. And he saith unto me, These are the true sayings of God.

THE BRIDE IS PRESENTED TO THE GROOM:

At the second coming of Jesus, He will bring together a new spiritual body of those who have been resurrected with a glorified body and this new body has never known sin and never was contaminated with the Adamic nature. The soul of each Believer is pure and clean and without sin because the atonement Jesus made for us cleansed us from all sin past and future and never to be remembered again. It is now possible for the New Testament Church, the Bride of Christ to be presented to Him without spot or wrinkle.

> Eph 5:27 That he might present it to himself a glorious church, not having spot, or wrinkle, or any such thing; but that it should be holy and without blemish.

The Bride of Christ is now said to be Holy and without blemish. The holy nature of the Saint of God is possible by being robed about with the righteousness of Christ Jesus our Lord. Another blessing Believers will possess is being a virgin of purity as we stand before the groom at the marriage of the Lamb. Every Christian will be precious to Jesus.

2Co 11:2 For I am jealous over you with godly jealousy: for I have espoused you to one husband, that I may present *you as* a chaste virgin to Christ.

The marriage of the New Testament Church to Jesus will unite us to Him to be one with Him as the marriage of husband and wife unites them together as one. The Bride of Christ will forever be with their Lord and never to be separated from His love and care for us.

Believers will not be married to their spouse in Heaven. Christ will be all that we need and desire; human companionship will not be needed to fulfill our lives with blessings.

Luk 20:34 And Jesus answering said unto them, The children of this world marry, and are given in marriage:

Luk 20:35 But they which shall be accounted worthy to obtain that world, and the resurrection from the dead, neither marry, nor are given in marriage:

OUR POSITION AS A BRIDE OF CHRIST:

Being made one with Christ brings many blessings to us that could only be given by the one who loved us and saved us to be His Bride.

Our first experience of knowing the Divine love of God is at the time we received Jesus as our Lord and Saviour. After the wedding in Heaven, Jesus will continue to love His bride with a divine pure love for all eternity that can only be express by deity.

Eph 2:6 And hath raised *us* up together, and made *us* sit together in heavenly *places* in Christ Jesus:

The Bride of Christ will be honored to share with and enjoy all of Heaven and glory that belongs to the Saviour. When a Christian couple marries today, the bride shares in every thing her groom possesses. In Heaven the bride will sit with Jesus in His throne and share the honor and glory of His rule from His throne. During the millennium Jesus will rule from the Throne of David in Jerusalem. Sitting with Jesus in His throne is an indication that the Bride will be given an exalted place of honor and dignity that belongs to the bridegroom.

> Rev 3:21 To him that overcometh will I grant to sit with me in my throne, even as I also overcame, and am set down with my Father in his throne.

Jesus will love His Bride forever; one age after another for all eternity this pure love called grace will never diminish. Jesus will express the riches of His grace to His Bride and by that bring greater glory to Him.

> **Eph 2:7** That in the ages to come he might shew the exceeding riches of his grace in *his* kindness toward us through Christ Jesus.

CHAPTER THREE

THE REVELATION OF JESUS:

For the past seven years of the Tribulation upon the earth the New Testament Saints have been in Heaven and the Tribulation is now completed. Jesus, the Kings of King and Lord of Lords, will leave Heaven and return to the earth to destroy the armies who have invaded Israel. The Bride of Christ with their mansion will follow their Lord on this journey to the earth and establish the Millennial Kingdom.

> Rev 19:14 And the armies *which were* in heaven followed him upon white horses, clothed in fine linen, white and clean.

> Rev 19:15 And out of his mouth goeth a sharp sword, that with it he should smite the nations: and he shall rule them with a rod of iron: and he treadeth the winepress of the fierceness and wrath of Almighty God.

> Rev 19:16 And he hath on *his* vesture and on his thigh a name written, KING OF KINGS, AND LORD OF LORDS.

THE ESTABLISHMENT OF THE MILLENNIUM:

Rev 21:10 And he carried me away in the spirit to a great and high mountain, and shewed me that great city, the holy Jerusalem, descending out of heaven from God,

For the next thousand years the Bride of Christ will live in their Holy City floating above this earth.

Isa 2:2 And it shall come to pass in the last days, *that* the mountain of the LORD'S house shall be established in the top of the mountains, and shall be exalted above the hills; and all nations shall flow unto it.

Isa 2:3 And many people shall go and say, Come ye, and let us go up to the mountain of the LORD, to the house of the God of Jacob; and he will teach us of his ways, and we will walk in his paths: for out of Zion shall go forth the law, and the word of the LORD from Jerusalem.

There is a curse upon this earth and the pure and holy city, with the Bride of Christ, will not be established upon this earth. After the millennial period is over a new earth will be brought in to replace the earth that now exists.

THOSE WHO GO INTO THE MILLENNIUM:

For a short period of time Jesus will reveal himself and the people who have lived through the Tribulation Period of seven years will have an opportunity to see Jesus in all of His glory. Those who see Jesus standing on the Mountain of Olives will have an opportunity to accept Him and be permitted to go into the Millennium with a human body. These tribulation saints have had to endure seven years of suffering inflicted by the anti Christ, and they have survived without taking the mark of the beast. Some will be saved during this time of persecution and are called tribulation saints. The tribulation

Saints who have endured to the end of this time of suffering will now enter into their rest.

Mat 24:11 And many false prophets shall rise, and shall deceive many.

Mat 24:12 And because iniquity shall abound, the love of many shall wax cold.

Mat 24:13 But he that shall endure unto the end, the same shall be saved.

Every human being who enters the Millennium will be those who have by faith trusted Jesus to save them by His grace. All nations that have been classified as goat nations and have hated Israel will be destroyed at the end of the Tribulation Period. Jesus will command that all goat nations perish by the word of His mouth.

Rev 19:15 And out of his mouth goeth a sharp sword, that with it he should smite the nations: and he shall rule them with a rod of iron: and he treadeth the winepress of the fierceness and wrath of Almighty God.

ANIMALS WILL GO INTO THE MILLENNIUM:

Domesticated animals and wild beast will all be tame and gentle. All animals will eat vegetation and never have a nature to kill or hurt any other creature including man. All species of animals will mingle together in restful peace and never drive other creatures from their midst. There is not any indication that any animal will be resurrected and be rejoined to those who had them as pets. Any animal that lives through the tribulation will continue to live and go into the millennium and will have a changed nature to be gentle.

Isa 11:6 The wolf also shall dwell with the lamb, and the leopard shall lie down with the kid; and the calf and the young lion and the fatling together; and a little child shall lead them.

Isa 11:7 And the cow and the bear shall feed; their young ones shall lie down together: and the lion shall eat straw like the ox.

Isa 11:8 And the sucking child shall play on the hole of the asp, and the weaned child shall put his hand on the cockatrice' den.

Isa 11:9 They shall not hurt nor destroy in all my holy mountain: for the earth shall be full of the knowledge of the LORD, as the waters cover the sea.

THE RESURRECTION OF OLD TESTAMENT SAINTS:

The Old Testament Saints who died and kept the Law by faith will be resurrected at the end of the Tribulation Period. Old Testament Saints will not be resurrected at the same time the Church is resurrected. The New Testament Church, the Bide of Christ, is taken to Heaven before the beginning of the Tribulation Period. The Church, living by faith, will be a chosen people to be the Bride of Christ. At the time of the Revelation of Jesus- at the end of the Tribulation Period-will be the resurrection of the Old Testament Saints. Those who died under the Law will, at this time, receive a glorified body like the body the New Testament Believers were given at the rapture of the Church.

Dan 12:1 And at that time shall Michael stand up, the great prince which standeth for the children of thy people: and there shall be a time of trouble, such as never was since there was a nation *even* to that same time: and at that time thy people shall be delivered, every one that shall be found written in the book.

Dan 12:2 And many of them that sleep in the dust of the earth shall awake, some to everlasting life, and some to shame *and* everlasting contempt.

Daniel records in his book that the time of the resurrection of Israel will be after a time of trouble. Some times this is said to be the time of Jacob's Trouble or the Tribulation Period of seven years.

All Old Testament Saints who are resurrected will dwell in the land of Israel promised to Abraham as he journeyed from Ur in Babylon to Egypt. Israel will now enjoy peace and live finally in all the land promised to Abraham for the first time in history.

The government established during the thousand years over the Earth will be a perfect rule of Jesus from the reestablished throne of David in Jerusalem. The Bride of Christ will rule over the human beings who enter the Millennium. The whole earth will be a perfect environment in which to live. Satan will be bound and cast in to the bottomless pit during this time, and he will not be able to deceive those human beings who have entered the Millennium.

Rev 20:1 And I saw an angel come down from heaven, having the key of the bottomless pit and a great chain in his hand.

Rev 20:2 And he laid hold on the dragon, that old serpent, which is the Devil, and Satan, and bound him a thousand years,

Rev 20:3 And cast him into the bottomless pit, and shut him up, and set a seal upon him, that he should deceive the nations no more, till the thousand years should be fulfilled: and after that he must be loosed a little season.

The people who survive the seven years of tribulation and accept Jesus as their Messiah will be saved and go into the Millennium. Since they are human beings they will still have the Adamic nature and will have to deal with the flesh that will still have a desire to sin. It will be the responsibility of the resurrected church to rule over these people and prevent them from sinful practices by removing temptation. The Bride of Christ will have the power to judge and stop all activity that is of a sinful nature.

The whole earth is now under the control of a perfect government and a clean environment. The Lord will give all human beings born to human parents one hundred years to accept Jesus as their Saviour and if not they will die and be lost.

Isa 65:19 And I will rejoice in Jerusalem, and joy in my people: and the voice of weeping shall be no more heard in her, nor the voice of crying.

Isa 65:20 There shall be no more thence an infant of days, nor an old man that hath not filled his days: for the child shall die an hundred years old; but the sinner *being* an hundred years old shall be accursed.

Those human beings who enter the millennium saved and have children who also trust Jesus as their Lord will live for the rest of the thousand years and then receive a glorified body suitable to enter the new earth the Lord will create.

THE CHILDREN BORN IN THE MILLENNIUM:

The human beings who survive the tribulation and go into the Millennium will have children. There will not be any sickness or pain during the thousand years of rule of the millennium.

Isa 33:24 And the inhabitant shall not say, I am sick: the people that dwell therein *shall be* forgiven *their* iniquity.

In a perfect environment for the thousand years there could be millions of children born to the natural parents. These Children will be given one hundred years to repent of their sins originating from their fallen Adamic nature they inherited from their parents. If the children who are born in the millennium do not accept Christ as their lord and Saviour, they will die and be lost.

> Isa 65:20 There shall be no more thence an infant of days, nor an old man that hath not filled his days: for the child shall die an hundred years old; but the sinner *being* an hundred years old shall be accursed.

The children who accept Jesus as their lord and Saviour will continue to live for the rest of the millennium and then be given a glorified body in which to live for eternity with the Lord in the New Heaven.

SATAN WILL BE BOUND DURING THE MILLENNIUM:

When the tribulation period is over, an angel from Heaven will come down to this earth and apprehend Satan and cast him into the bottomless pit. The angel will also put a seal upon the prison, and Satan will not be able to escape and return to the earth. For the next one thousand years Satan cannot tempt anyone to sin.

> **Rev 20:1** And I saw an angel come down from heaven, having the key of the bottomless pit and a great chain in his hand.

> Rev 20:2 And he laid hold on the dragon, that old serpent, which is the Devil, and Satan, and bound him a thousand years,

> Rev 20:3 And cast him into the bottomless pit, and shut him up, and set a seal upon him, that he should deceive the nations no more, till the thousand years should be fulfilled: and after that he must be loosed a little season.

Children born to the parents who go into the Millennium will be born with the Adamic nature and still have a desire to sin and live after the desires of the flesh. There will not be any sickness and suffering during the Millennium and as a result billions of people could be living at the end of the Millennium. These children will not enjoy the restrictions placed upon them to live according to Christian conduct. Satan will be released from the bottomless pit at the end of the millennium. The children who have not accepted Jesus as their Lord in this perfect environment will be deceived by Satan and be led to overthrow the Millennial Kingdom. The conflict that ensues, and led by Satan, is called the Battle of Gog and Magog. God will end this war by destroying those who believed and followed Satan with fire coming out of Heaven.

Rev 20:7 And when the thousand years are expired, Satan shall be loosed out of his prison,

Rev 20:8 And shall go out to deceive the nations which are in the four quarters of the earth, Gog and Magog, to gather them together to battle: the number of whom *is* as the sand of the sea.

Rev 20:9 And they went up on the breadth of the earth, and compassed the camp of the saints about, and the beloved city: and fire came down from God out of heaven, and devoured them.

Rev 20:10 And the devil that deceived them was cast into the lake of fire and brimstone, where the beast and the false prophet *are*, and shall be tormented day and night for ever and ever.

Satan is finally cast into the Lake of fire and will never be released to tempt anyone in all of eternity.

CHAPTER FOUR

THE NEW HEAVEN AND NEW EARTH:

W hen the Thousand Years have ended the Lord Jesus will destroy this old earth which is still under the curse that occurred when Adam and Eve sinned in the Garden of Eden. The earth and all of the stellar Heaven will vanish which could be possible when Jesus commands all atoms to collide and burn up all the material substance on this earth.

> 2Pe 3:10 But the day of the Lord will come as a thief in the night; in the which the heavens shall pass away with a great noise, and the elements shall melt with fervent heat, the earth also and the works that are therein shall be burned up.
>
> 2Pe 3:11 *Seeing* then *that* all these things shall be dissolved, what manner *of persons* ought ye to be in *all* holy conversation and godliness,
>
> 2Pe 3:12 Looking for and hasting unto the coming of the day of God, wherein the heavens being on fire shall be dissolved, and the elements shall melt with fervent heat?

2Pe 3:13 Nevertheless we, according to his promise, look for new heavens and a new earth, wherein dwelleth righteousness.

The new earth will be perfect, different, beautiful, and will no longer be cursed like our world is today. When the new earth is created the Holy City where the Bride of Christ dwells will now be settled down on a new world suitable to receive the home of the Bride of Christ. Jesus will have His throne in the midst of the Holy City, the New Jerusalem, dwelling with the Bride of Christ, the new Testament Church.

The Greek word, (kainos), translated new means something recently made and never used.

Rev 21:1 And I saw a new heaven and a new earth: for the first heaven and the first earth were passed away; and there was no more sea.

The Prophet Isaiah wrote that the new heaven and earth will remain before the Lord forever and will be created in the future at the end of the Millennium.

Isa 66:22 For as the new heavens and the new earth, which I will make, shall remain before me, saith the LORD, so shall your seed and your name remain.

THE BEAUTY OF THE NEW EARTH:

John describes the beauty of the New Jerusalem as that of a bride who has done everything to make herself beautiful for her groom. The Heavenly City is a prepared dwelling place for the Bride of Christ. The one who prepares the eternal home for the bride is the Saviour and Groom of the New Testament Saints.

Rev 21:2 And I John saw the holy city, new Jerusalem, coming down from God out of heaven, prepared as a bride adorned for her husband.

Jesus himself will forever be with the bride of Christ and dwell together in the Holy City. Rev. 21:3 tells us that the tabernacle of God, tabernacle means a swelling place, is Jesus dwelling in His resurrected body who is God in the fullness of Deity. The eternal existence of Jesus the very God will be eternal and will forever be with believers in Heaven.

Rev 1:18 I *am* he that liveth, and was dead; and, behold, I am alive for evermore, Amen; and have the keys of hell and of death.

THE BRIDE IS BLESSED AND COMFORTED:

All problems experienced in this life will never be known in Heaven. Tears of grief will never be shed because there will never be a soul disturbed neither will there be an aching heart.

Rev 21:4 And God shall wipe away all tears from their eyes; and there shall be no more death, neither sorrow, nor crying, neither shall there be any more pain: for the former things are passed away.

During the Millennium some of the human beings who are born during the thousand years may die after living for one hundred years because they refuse to accept Jesus as their Lord. Every one who enters the eternal age will have a glorified body and will never die. This verse also teaches us there will never be any circumstances developing to cause sorrow. The glorified body is perfect and will never change to become old and subject to sickness; as a result, pain will not be known for all eternity. The physical and emotional problems we know today will forever be a thing of the past.

THE ASSURANCE AND BLESSINGS:

Rev. 21:5 was written to reassure us that things may seem too good to be true, but these things are most certainly true and dependable. Rev 21:5 And he that sat upon the throne said, Behold, I make all things new. And he said unto me, Write: for these words are true and faithful.

When the Lord Jesus makes a new planet for the Saints of God, it will be new to the extent that it will be a drastic change and will not be like the earth is today. Satan will be cast into Hell, and his influence of evil will never again be known in the new earth. Satan has brought into this world death and all the sufferings man has endured; for the first time evil is destroyed forever.

Another comfort for us is written in verse six when Jesus "proclaims it is done;" the Greek reveals they are come to pass. The Alpha and Omega is an illustration that indicates Jesus is the eternal God who existed before all things and will still exist when things pass away.

Those who thirst, or have any desire, will be completely satisfied because the Lord Jesus will be all we need for a perfect existence with Him.

Rev 21:6 And he said unto me, It is done. I am Alpha and Omega, the beginning and the end. I will give unto him that is athirst of the fountain of the water of life freely.

When the Bride is with Jesus in Heaven and is athirst (or having any desire) will find satisfaction and fulfillment completely in our source of comfort- the Lord Jesus.

When the new earth comes into existence, all who have died with faith in the atonement to save them will dwell together. The faithful of all ages, including the Old Testament and New Testament Believers, will have full access to all we have inherited in the new earth. The eternal God will have a pure relationship with all believers who dwell in the New Heaven. Being considered as a son of God is to have the care and blessing of a family member by God forever.

Rev 21:7 He that overcometh shall inherit all things; and I will be his God, and he shall be my son.

Those who overcome are those who have achieved the victory over the world, the flesh, and the devil. These saints of God receive their inheritance of the mansion the Lord Jesus has prepared for His Bride, the New Testament Church. The God who is deity and the creator of all things is our Heavenly Father. In a unique sense we are a family and looked upon as a son of God the Father.

An Angel instructed John to join him and get a view of the Bride of Christ who is now made perfect, they will received their glorified body at the resurrection when Jesus calls believers to come forth from their grave. The Bride John saw was clothed in white robes representing purity belonging to the glorified body our Lord calls forth from the grave.

Rev 21:9 And there came unto me one of the seven angels which had the seven vials full of the seven last plagues, and talked with me, saying, Come hither, I will shew thee the bride, the Lamb's wife.

THE HOLY JERUSALEM SETTLES UPON THE NEW EARTH:

During the time of the millennium our Heavenly Home will be hovering above the earth.

Isa 2:2 And it shall come to pass in the last days, *that* the mountain of the LORD'S house shall be established in the top of the mountains, and shall be exalted above the hills; and all nations shall flow unto it.

For the past one thousand years the bride of Christ has ruled the earth from the New Jerusalem that floated above the earth. Jesus has His throne inside the Holy City we dwell in and anyone needing to have an audience with the Lord would leave this earth and enter the city floating above the earth.

Isa 2:3 And many people shall go and say, Come ye, and let us go up to the mountain of the LORD, to the house of the

God of Jacob; and he will teach us of his ways, and we will walk in his paths: for out of Zion shall go forth the law, and the word of the LORD from Jerusalem.

The time has come for the city Jesus has prepared for us to have its foundation upon the new earth. God will not permit His holy City to settle upon any world that has a curse upon it. The new earth God will create, after the millennium is over, will not have the curse upon it as the original earth had.

Rev 22:3 And there shall be no more curse: but the throne of God and of the Lamb shall be in it; and his servants shall serve him:

The size of the New Jerusalem is at least twelve hundred miles square.

Rev 21:16 And the city lieth foursquare, and the length is as large as the breadth: and he measured the city with the reed, twelve thousand furlongs. The length and the breadth and the height of it are equal.

The throne of Jesus is located in the center of our heavenly city where Jesus will rule all of the new heaven and earth. A clear and pure river of water will flow from the throne of Jesus for the distance of more than six hundred miles.

Rev 22:1 And he shewed me a pure river of water of life, clear as crystal, proceeding out of the throne of God and of the Lamb.

Along the banks of the beautiful river trees of life will be growing twelve different varieties of fruit. The trees bearing fruit every month indicates the trees will yield ripe fruit all the time. Eating the leaves on the tree of life will give those who eat immortality; and they will never die because the curse of death will be removed.

Rev 22:2 In the midst of the street of it, and on either side of the river, *was there* the tree of life, which bare twelve *manner of* fruits, *and* yielded her fruit every month: and the leaves of the tree *were* for the healing of the nations.

Rev 22:3 And there shall be no more curse: but the throne of God and of the Lamb shall be in it; and his servants shall serve him:

Ezekiel gives more information about the trees that grow along the sides of the river in Heaven. All of the fruit on the trees are for food that may be eaten by those in Heaven. It seems obvious that we will enjoy eating food in Heaven. The leaf will not die and the trees will forever produce food for us to enjoy. A different variety of fruit is grown each month and said to be new fruit. The leaves are for medicine like the tree of life that was originally given in the Garden of Eden. Every person who eats of the tree of life will live forever. In Heaven the same type of tree will give us life forever.

Eze 47:12 And by the river upon the bank thereof, on this side and on that side, shall grow all trees for meat, whose leaf shall not fade, neither shall the fruit thereof be consumed: it shall bring forth new fruit according to his months, because their waters they issued out of the sanctuary: and the fruit thereof shall be for meat, and the leaf thereof for medicine.

THE BEAUTY OF THE NEW JERUSALEM:

The Holy Spirit made it possible for John to see the New Jerusalem as it ascends out of Heaven to hover above the earth during the Millennium. John also saw the glory of God and described the light of God as it was reflected from the jewels like a jasper stone. The light he saw was clear as crystal which tells us that there were not any impurities in the light that came from God.

Rev 21:10 And he carried me away in the spirit to a great and high mountain, and shewed me that great city, the holy Jerusalem, descending out of heaven from God,

Rev 21:11 Having the glory of God: and her light *was* like unto a stone most precious, even like a jasper stone, clear as crystal;

The city in which the Bride of Christ will dwell will be in length between 1378 to 1500 miles square.

Rev 21:16 And the city lieth foursquare, and the length is as large as the breadth: and he measured the city with the reed, twelve thousand furlongs. The length and the breadth and the height of it are equal.

Rev 21:17 And he measured the wall thereof, an hundred *and* forty *and* four cubits, *according to* the measure of a man, that is, of the angel.

There will be three gates on each of the four walls entering to the streets in the Holy City. The twelve foundations of the wall will have the names of the twelve apostles recorded in them.

Rev 21:14 And the wall of the city had twelve foundations, and in them the names of the twelve apostles of the Lamb.

The height of the wall surrounding the Holy City is about 216 feet high. The wall is most often used in Biblical days to display strength and grandeur of the city. The wall was also a protective guard for all who dwell therein.

Rev 21:17 And he measured the wall thereof, an hundred *and* forty *and* four cubits, *according to* the measure of a man, that is, of the angel.

The wall was of Jasper as the color of a rainbow. The city made of gold like clear glass. The gold is like clear glass which does not have any impurities.

Rev 21:18 And the building of the wall of it was *of* jasper: and the city *was* pure gold, like unto clear glass.

The jewels decorating the wall are beautiful in that they reflect all different colors of the spectrum believers can now see with their glorified bodies. Each gate is one pearl in size leading into the streets of pure gold. Again, this gold is described as it were transparent glass denoting this type of glass is without any impurities. The gold is not transparent but pure without any impurities.

Rev 21:21 And the twelve gates *were* twelve pearls; every several gate was of one pearl: and the street of the city *was* pure gold, as it were transparent glass.

There will be no need to go to a temple in the New Jerusalem to worship because God dwells with us. Within our mansion the Lord will forever be with us and worship will be a continual activity for those who dwell there.

Rev 21:22 And I saw no temple therein: for the Lord God Almighty and the Lamb are the temple of it.

Any place where sin is found there is darkness. In the new Heaven and Earth sin does not exist in the presence of God and as a result there is always light because there is no darkness.

Every person from any part of this world who is saved will be in the new Heaven and enjoy the blessings of being with their Saviour. The Saints are recorded as kings in Heaven because they will rule and reign with Christ. The nations or Gentiles will bring greater glory and honor to the Lord Jesus for extending His love and grace to save them who deserved only condemnation and Hell.

Rev 21:24 And the nations of them which are saved shall walk in the light of it: and the kings of the earth do bring their glory and honour into it.

There will never be any thing to fear as a result of sin and crime. Doors or gates will never need to be shut or locked to keep out criminals. Satan and all of the fallen angels will be in the lake of fire who would desire to hurt and destroy. Fear is no longer an emotion that causes anxiety for those in Heaven. People who are now in Heaven are those who received Jesus as their Lord and Saviour, by faith, and by that had their name written in the Lamb's book of life.

Rev 21:25 And the gates of it shall not be shut at all by day: for there shall be no night there.

Rev 21:26 And they shall bring the glory and honour of the nations into it.

Rev 21:27 And there shall in no wise enter into it any thing that defileth, neither *whatsoever* worketh abomination, or *maketh* a lie: but they which are written in the Lamb's book of life.

THE SAINTS OF GOD WILL DWELL IN PEACE FOREVER:

Jesus will be ruling from the throne located inside the Holy City. All instruments of war will be destroyed and will never be needed again. The Prince of Peace brings peace to all His Children dwelling in the new world.

Isa 2:4 And he shall judge among the nations, and shall rebuke many people: and they shall beat their swords into plowshares, and their spears into pruninghooks: nation shall not lift up sword against nation, neither shall they learn war any more.

Believers have often wished that they could have seen the Lord Jesus when He was with His disciples. For all eternity to come believers will see the Lord Jesus and see Him as He looked while on earth. To see the Lord's face suggest we will have access to Him and He will meet our every need. The name of Jesus in our forehead indicates His ownership of us by being united to Him as our Bridegroom.

Rev 22:4 And they shall see his face; and his name *shall be* in their foreheads.

THE LORD GOD IS THE LIGHT OF THE NEW EARTH:

There never will be a moment of time when darkness will exist anywhere in the new Heaven. The Lord Jesus will continually dwell with us in the New Earth and darkness does not exist in the presence of Deity. All the Saints of all ages will abide in the delight of the pure light of God and never become tired or need to sleep, because, our glorified bodies will never become exhausted and need rest.

Rev 22:5 And there shall be no night there; and they need no candle, neither light of the sun; for the Lord God giveth them light: and they shall reign for ever and ever.

Saints of all nations will spend all eternity worshiping and giving glory to Jesus who saved them. No one will ever become tired of worship because Jesus will forever be worthy of our praise. When the inhabitants of Heaven see Jesus sitting upon His throne and view the splendor and glory; they will forever realize Jesus is deserving of our praise and worship.

Rev 21:24 And the nations of them which are saved shall walk in the light of it: and the kings of the earth do bring their glory and honour into it.

Jesus will forever inform us of His divine love and care for us even while we were still living upon this earth. The expressions of love Jesus uses when He gathers us around Him in Heaven will forever thrill us with joy and blessings of comfort only Jesus can give to His Believers.

Eph 2:6 And hath raised *us* up together, and made *us* sit together in heavenly *places* in Christ Jesus:

Eph 2:7 That in the ages to come he might shew the exceeding riches of his grace in *his* kindness toward us through Christ Jesus.

JESUS PRAYED FOR HIS BELIEVERS BEFORE HE WAS CRUCIFIED:

Jesus wanted to reveal to the Disciples the extent of His love for them before He died on the cross. The twelve disciples needed to be reassured that the Father also loved them by trusting His Son as their Saviour.

Joh 16:27 For the Father himself loveth you, because ye have loved me, and have believed that I came out from God.

Jesus was walking east toward a garden named Gethsemane to pray a short time before Judas would betray Him and there be taken by the Roman soldiers. Jesus was now near the Eastern Gate where He prayed for them and for the New Testament Church. When Jesus prayed, He revealed how much He loved us and His desire for us to be with Him in Heaven. At the moment we are saved, the bride of Christ is made to be one with Him like the relationship that exists between Jesus and the Father.

Joh 17:21 That they all may be one; as thou, Father, *art* in me, and I in thee, that they also may be one in us: that the world may believe that thou hast sent me.

Joh 17:22 And the glory which thou gavest me I have given them; that they may be one, even as we are one:

Near the end of His prayer Jesus again prayed to God that he was eagerly waiting to have His bride, the church, to be with him, so He will be able to let us see the fullness of the light of His glory. Paul described the light he saw when he looked into heaven and saw the risen Lord Jesus appearing as a light brighter than the sun. Those who are in Heaven will behold the glory of Jesus as the light reflects splendor, dignity, praise, and perfection of Deity. We who are with our Lord Jesus will never become tired of seeing the glory of Him who saved us by His grace.

1Jo 3:2 Beloved, now are we the sons of God, and it doth not yet appear what we shall be: but we know that, when he shall appear, we shall be like him; for we shall see him as he is.

BOOK TWO

THE LOST PERSON'S JOURNEY
INTO ETERNITY

CHAPTER ONE

PHYSICALLY ALIVE AND SPIRITUALLY DEAD:

God created mankind with a will to do whatever he chooses to do without any coercion from God. Man can freely choose to trust Jesus to save him or reject Jesus as their Saviour. Jesus made the only atonement that forgives all the sins of the world and any person may be saved if they by faith invite Jesus into their life as their Lord and Master. Every one who reaches the age of accountability must accept the Lord Jesus to save them or be lost. At the moment we trust Jesus to save us by faith the Holy Spirit gives spiritual life to our soul and births us into God's Spiritual Family.

THE LOST PERSONS DIES ALONE:

When a lost person dies, they experience a death of dying alone and without any hope of going to Heaven. When a Christian dies, they do not have a fear of death because the Lord is with them. There will not be any angels to accompany the lost person during their death experience. The lost person does have something to fear by entering into an eternal existence without having a Saviour who loves and cares for them.

> Psa 23:4 Yea, though I walk through the valley of the shadow of death, I will fear no evil: for thou *art* with me; thy rod and thy staff they comfort me.

Jesus gave an illustration of the difference between the death of the rich man, representing the lost person, and that of Lazarus who was a saved person. Lazarus died and was carried to Heaven by an angel and was comforted. The rich man, who was lost, died and went down alone into a place of torment. Being in torment indicates suffering and no comfort, not even a drop of water. The lost person was also well alert asked Abraham to permit some one, from that place, to go back on earth and warn his brothers to escape coming to this place. The rich man wanted his brothers to have someone to instruct them how to be saved by trusting by faith a proper atonement Jesus made for their sins. Jesus said that this mission from Hades back to earth was impossible; After some person enters Hades there is no possible way to escape its punishment for any reason.

Luk 16:22 And it came to pass, that the beggar died, and was carried by the angels into Abraham's bosom: the rich man also died, and was buried;

Luk 16:23 And in hell he lift up his eyes, being in torments, and seeth Abraham afar off, and Lazarus in his bosom.

Luk 16:24 And he cried and said, Father Abraham, have mercy on me, and send Lazarus, that he may dip the tip of his finger in water, and cool my tongue; for I am tormented in this flame.

Luk 16:25 But Abraham said, Son, remember that thou in thy lifetime receivedst thy good things, and likewise Lazarus evil things: but now he is comforted, and thou art tormented.

Luk 16:26 And beside all this, between us and you there is a great gulf fixed: so that they which would pass from hence to you cannot; neither can they pass to us, that *would come* from thence.

THE LOST PERSON EXPERIENCES SUFFERING AT DEATH:

Paul gives us much information about death and what happens to our body. Believers do not experience a sting of death and they also have a victory over death in that the grave will not keep us beyond the time of their resurrection to be with the Lord. It is understood that the sting experienced is pain for the Lost when they die. The Greek understanding of the word sting is that of a prick or goad. It is also considered as an injection of poison that brings pain when a bee stings some one who is an intruder into their territory.

1Co 15:55 O death, where *is* thy sting? O grave, where *is* thy victory?

1Co 15:56 The sting of death *is* sin; and the strength of sin *is* the law.

1Co 15:57 But thanks *be* to God, which giveth us the victory through our Lord Jesus Christ.

HADES WILL EXIST UNTIL THE GREAT WHITE THRONE JUDGEMENT:

Before the resurrection of Jesus from the dead all who died were kept in one of two compartments in a place called Hades, but some times it is translated in English as hell, a place of suffering. Every person who dies without having their sins forgiven, by the atonement required by God, will go to Hades. When Jesus died on the cross, He made the atonement that would forgive every sin of any person who trust Him by faith to save them. The Old Testament Saints were held in the compartment called Abraham's bosom. The place of rest in Hades was divided with a gulf, or space, that separated the saints and the lost people from leaving their area and crossing over to the other compartment.

Luk 16:22 And it came to pass, that the beggar died, and was carried by the angels into Abraham's bosom: the rich man also died, and was buried;

Luk 16:23 And in hell he lift up his eyes, being in torments, and seeth Abraham afar off, and Lazarus in his bosom.

Luk 16:24 And he cried and said, Father Abraham, have mercy on me, and send Lazarus, that he may dip the tip of his finger in water, and cool my tongue; for I am tormented in this flame.

Luk 16:25 But Abraham said, Son, remember that thou in thy lifetime receivedst thy good things, and likewise Lazarus evil things: but now he is comforted, and thou art tormented.

Luk 16:26 And beside all this, between us and you there is a great gulf fixed: so that they which would pass from hence to you cannot; neither can they pass to us, that *would come* from thence.

On Easter Sunday morning Jesus went into Abraham's bosom of Hades, called Paradise, and delivered those saints out of the place of keeping. Jesus took all of the Old Testament Saints to the third Heaven where God dwells. Jesus appeared to Mary at the tomb to inform her and the disciples He was resurrected and now on a mission to deliver the Old Testament Saints to Heaven; Jesus asked Mary not to hold Him and delay His mission of delivering the Saints to Heaven.

Joh 20:16 Jesus saith unto her, Mary. She turned herself, and saith unto him, Rabboni; which is to say, Master.

Joh 20:17 Jesus saith unto her, Touch me not; for I am not yet ascended to my Father: but go to my brethren, and say unto them, I ascend unto my Father, and your Father; and *to* my God, and your God.

Joh 20:18 Mary Magdalene came and told the disciples that she had seen the Lord, and *that* he had spoken these things unto her.

When Jesus went to the place of comfort, in Hades, to take the Saints out of Abraham's bosom He descended into that place, called paradise, where captives were held and then ascended up into Heaven which would indicate that the location of Hades is some where in the earth.

Eph 4:8 Wherefore he saith, When he ascended up on high, he led captivity captive, and gave gifts unto men.

Eph 4:9 (Now that he ascended, what is it but that he also descended first into the lower parts of the earth?

Eph 4:10 He that descended is the same also that ascended up far above all heavens, that he might fill all things.)

After Jesus took the Saints out of Abraham's bosom, the place of Paradise no longer exists there and Hades was enlarged to contain the lost in this place of torment.

Isa 5:14 Therefore hell hath enlarged herself, and opened her mouth without measure: and their glory, and their multitude, and their pomp, and he that rejoiceth, shall descend into it.

Isa 5:15 And the mean man shall be brought down, and the mighty man shall be humbled, and the eyes of the lofty shall be humbled:

Hades will continue to hold captive all the lost of all ages until the judgment at the Great White Throne, which will take place after the millennium is over.

THE LOST IN HADES ARE ALIVE AND CONCIOUS:

Jesus informs us that the rich man who was lost cried out to Abraham to send Lazarus with a little water to cool his parched tongue. There is physical hurt and suffering in torment in Hades.

Luk 16:24 And he cried and said, Father Abraham, have mercy on me, and send Lazarus, that he may dip the tip of his finger in water, and cool my tongue; for I am tormented in this flame.

The lost person also realized that he had five brothers still alive back on earth and he did not want them to come to Hades and suffer with him.

Luk 16:27 Then he said, I pray thee therefore, father, that thou wouldest send him to my father's house:

Luk 16:28 For I have five brethren; that he may testify unto them, lest they also come into this place of torment.

Luk 16:29 Abraham saith unto him, They have Moses and the prophets; let them hear them.

Luk 16:30 And he said, Nay, father Abraham: but if one went unto them from the dead, they will repent.

Luk 16:31 And he said unto him, If they hear not Moses and the prophets, neither will they be persuaded, though one rose from the dead.

THE GREAT WHITE THRONE JUDGMENT:

Soon, after the rapture of the church, the seven years of the tribulation will start; after that time there will be the millennial rule and reign of Christ for one thousand years upon this earth. Following this time Jesus will set up a throne of judgment some where in space. All the lost people of all ages will be called out of Hades to be judged.

The lost souls who are called to be judged are those who refused to accept the Lord Jesus as their Lord and Saviour. They actually were saying to God the Father they cared nothing about His Son and He was not worthy of their time or interest. Lost people who are to be judged never considered Jesus to be worthy of their worship. God created humanity to worship Him. Those who trust Jesus to save them worship Him at the time they are saved. Every lost person of all ages will now worship Jesus at the Great White Throne Judgment. At this time it is too late to be forgiven and go to Heaven. The reason for being born will be achieved as the sinner bows before Deity and worships Him when they realize Jesus is worthy of their worship.

Rom 14:11 For it is written, *As* I live, saith the Lord, every knee shall bow to me, and every tongue shall confess to God.

Most likely no human beings have ever fully understood the majesty and glory of the Son of God. When the lost person looks upon the Lord Jesus in the fullness of His Glory, they will realize for the first time the serious sad mistake they have made by rejecting God's Son to be their Lord and Saviour.

As the lost souls, who are now given a body that cannot be destroyed even by fire, are called to stand before the great white throne judgment will see the earth recede from their sight as they are caught up into space.

Rev 20:11 And I saw a great white throne, and him that sat on it, from whose face the earth and the heaven fled away; and there was found no place for them.

The Scriptures record that the small and great will stand before Jesus who is God; this tells us that no one will escape this judgment. The books containing the record of their sins and rejection of Jesus as their Saviour will be seen as a written confession of what they did on earth. Every lost person, who reviews their record, cannot deny their life long record of sinning. When that Lost person beholds the radiance of glory of the countenance of Jesus, they will be fully convinced they deserve nothing less than banishment into the lake of fire. The lord Jesus will not have to condemn any soul to the lake of fire because they are already condemned by their record.

> Joh 3:18 He that believeth on him is not condemned: but he that believeth not is condemned already, because he hath not believed in the name of the only begotten Son of God.

It is not their sins that condemn a lost person to the lake of fire. Those being judged are lost, because, they did not receive Jesus as their Saviour and the atonement He made for them on the cross. Their record of sins committed will determine the degree of mental anguish they endure for all eternity.

The physical punishment of the lake of fire will be the same for all. There is punishment in the area of the mental, which is seen by those weeping and gnashing of teeth, which results from a mental state of anguish. Every lost person will relive and remember the suffering they caused while they committed their crimes and regret what they did. The Bible often indicates the lost will remember as they exist in the lake of fire.

> Mat 8:12 But the children of the kingdom shall be cast out into outer darkness: there shall be weeping and gnashing of teeth.

> Luk 16:25 But Abraham said, Son, remember that thou in thy lifetime receivedst thy good things, and likewise Lazarus evil things: but now he is comforted, and thou art tormented.

THE LAKE OF FIRE WILL BE CREATED FOR SATAN:

The first two occupants to be cast into Hell, the eternal lake of fire, will be the Beast and false prophet. Satan organized his rule on the earth to be by an unholy trinity of Satan, the beast, and false prophet. Sometimes the anti Christ is called the first beast and the anti Holy Spirit is called the second beast. Near the end of the tribulation period, the beast and false prophet will be the first two occupants to be cast into hell.

> Rev 19:20 And the beast was taken, and with him the false prophet that wrought miracles before him, with which he deceived them that had received the mark of the beast, and them that worshipped his image. These both were cast alive into a lake of fire burning with brimstone.

The next fallen angel to be cast into hell will be Satan, the anti God. This event will take place at the end of the millennium. Never again will the unholy trinity tempt man and bring death and sorrow for the inhabitants of the new earth.

> Rev 20:10 And the devil that deceived them was cast into the lake of fire and brimstone, where the beast and the false prophet *are*, and shall be tormented day and night for ever and ever.

The lake of fire was only created to punish Satan and all of the fallen angels who followed him. Originally, the lake of fire called hell was not intended for the abode of human beings. At the time of the great white throne judgment, there will be only two places where any one can spend eternity. If a human being refuses to accept Jesus as their Lord and Saviour, and by that refuse to qualify to be admitted into Heaven there is no other place the lost souls can go but into the lake of fire. Everyone who goes to the lake of fire will go there against the will of God our Father. God is not willing that any soul should be lost and finally go to Hell; it is Gods will that all be saved and go to Heaven.

> 2Pe 3:9 The Lord is not slack concerning his promise, as some men count slackness; but is longsuffering to us-ward, not willing that any should perish, but that all should come to repentance.

The heart of God is seen by His appeal for everyone to accept His son as their Saviour, by faith, to save them and He does not desire that any human being be lost and go to hell.

Rev 22:17 And the Spirit and the bride say, Come. And let him that heareth say, Come. And let him that is athirst come. And whosoever will, let him take the water of life freely.

Printed in the United States
135173LV00002B/1/P

9 781607 911883